TWELVE REASONS WHY
BLACK PEOPLE
ARE LOSING IN LIFE

By
Donele "Casino" Bailey

12 REASONS WHY
BLACK
PEOPLE
ARE LOSING IN LIFE

by
Donele "Casino" Bailey

MP

MOCY PUBLISHING, LLC

Detroit, Michigan

12 Reasons Why – Black People Are Losing In Life
ISBN 978-0-9834700-0-7
Copyright © 2012 by Donele "Casino" Bailey

Published by Mocy Publishing, LLC.
Website: www.mocypublishing.com
Email: info@mocypublishing.com
Phone: (313) 436-6944

by
Donele "Casino" Bailey

Transcribed by
Semaja Bailey

Published by
Mocy Publishing, LLC

This book is also available at
most of your major book retail stores.

Discover other titles by
Donele "Casino" Bailey at Mocypublishing.com

Acknowledgements 7

Introduction 8

Reason 1

WE LACK EDUCATION 10

Reason 2

WE HAVE TOO MUCH PRIDE 18

Reason 3

WE LACK OUR RESPONSIBILITIES 23

Reason 4

WE'RE VERY MATERIALISTIC 29

Reason 5

WE HAVE NO UNDERSTANDING

OF OUR HISTORY 35

Reason 6

WE DON'T RESPECT SEX 41

Reason 7

EVERYONE WANTS TO BE A

CELEBRITY OR BOSS 47

Reason 8

WE DON'T RESPECT EACH OTHER 53

Reason 9

MOST OF US HAVE NO

SPIRITUAL CONNECTION 59

Reason 10

WE DON'T CARE ABOUT OUR HEALTH................... 66

Reason 11

WE DON'T GIVE EACH OTHER SUPPORT 72

Reason 12

WE HAVE SELFISH BEHAVIORS................................ 79

Acknowledgements

Besides my lord and savior "Jesus Christ," I would like to acknowledge a few people who inspired me on my journey to becoming a better black man.

To my beautiful children, Don'te, Dillon, Donele Jr., Semaja, and Dava'Reyon, who supported me and loved me unconditionally. To my mother Marie Bailey who did the best she could to raise me without a father. To my siblings India, Scott, Sheria, and Fuchsia who kept me in their prayers. To Mikesha Turner, Tamara Hill, Charnell Hargrove, Nicole Hawkins, and Marcie White who showed me that a black man is nothing without a strong black women. To Lamont Williams who showed me what true family is really about. To Flex Stevenson, who properly introduced me to Jesus Christ. To a person not with us today, but whom I consider a father when he was alive, my grandfather Oliver "OJ" James Evans. To the people who supported me when I got home, Frank "Yello" Harvest Jr., DeCarlos Stewart, Samantha Jones, Malachi Jones, LaToya Lewis, Patrice Williams, Meko Starr and Natasha Sanders. And lastly, to my uncle Andre "Bay-Bay" Bailey for holding me down and keeping a smile on my face through really tough times. Thank you all!

Introduction

My name is Donele "Casino" Bailey and I'm a music producer/executive from Detroit, Michigan. Although music is my passion, my biggest passion is constructing ways to help my people (black people) in life. For many years me and my people have struggled personally, socially, spiritually, and financially. And with my accomplishments, I felt it was only necessary to contribute something to my people that might change these struggles. This book was also very special for me to write because it came straight from my heart. This book is not in any way directed to offend any person but to up lift a falling race. These vows and opinions are solemnly from my point of view.

As I looked in the mirror and walked outside, I see a pattern of the things that make us (black people) all question ourselves. Why are our neighborhoods filled with guns and drugs? Why are our children falling behind in school? Why do we account for most of the prison population? Why are we dying at such an early age? Why are we killing each other over products companies' mass produce? These are just some of the issues we (black people) struggle with in our homes and communities. And with so many problems my people face, it got me to the point where I had to express myself.

Anyway, I hope this book will change your life and make you a better person as it changed me. Because with all the problems we (black people) have to deal with daily, sometimes the answer is right in our hands. So open your mind and open your soul and let this book guide you into understanding how far you really could go in life.

Reason 1

WE LACK EDUCATION

This is one of the first issues I had to address for multiple reasons. The first issue I'll start with is at home. I think most black families lack to education their children at the early ages. Educating children at an early age should be a standard. Leaving a child in front of the television screen to watch Sesame Street while the parents sneak to the bedroom for sex shouldn't be a form of educating the child. Non-educational video games should also be disqualified. The most important task for a parent is to be interactive with their child. What the parent teaches the child is even more important. For example, if you are playing a game with your child and you teach the child how to cheat, more likely that child will grow up to be a crook.

One major problem in most black households is that the parents lack knowledge on how to educate the child, which may have started from the parent not being educated while they were young. I've been in black households were the parents cursed their kids, used drugs in front of their kids, and even made sexual gestures in front of their kids. What most black parents don't realize is that children are like sponges. They absorb everything they see and hear. So when you tell a child "you ain't shit and won't amount to nothing in life," the child starts to behave in that manner because the information is coming from the parent.

Black parents must understand that it's really important to educate your child correctly by setting examples. Meaning, don't tell the child don't smoke and 5 minutes later you fire up a Newport. Another thing I hate is when a parent tells a child not to do something and don't explain why. How can a child relate to a subject without an illustration? Also don't be afraid to tell your child you're a little behind on rent this month. Explain to them why the lights and gas in the house is much more needed than a pair of Jordan shoes you promised him or her. Always remember, education starts at the early stages.

My second issue concerning education is about the public school systems black parents allow their kids to attend. I can remember when I was in the 5th grade years ago, the books we had to use were out dated, secondary to suburban school books, and the books even smelled like mildew. These days' things haven't changed much. Now I know the biggest problem with switching schools is trying to obtain financial assists, but there are also other options we can approach. So by analyzing the circumstances, the only way to change this situation is by getting more involved with the public school systems. And yes it sounds easy, but it's hard to accomplish when most black families don't even like to come to parent/teacher conference meetings. I can't even remember when my mother came to one of those meetings other than me acting out in school.

Black people we most get out and get involved with our children's education. Not to say your child is not educated, but lacking education to fulfill the child's full potential. For example, when I was 9 years old, my mother saw how passionate I was with music and dance. The thing was, my mother didn't have the proper education to nurture my talent. So temporally my dreams were lose, but by the grace of God I received the education to further my talent many years later. This is why education is so important. Getting involved and educating ourselves about our child's goals and talents should be a necessity. A lot of black kids lose their dreams because of this issue. We should also let them know how education plays a major role in whatever they're trying to accomplish. Rather they want to be a police officer, a basketball player, or even president of the United States, education is the key component for making that dream a reality.

The third issue concerning the lack of education is in the business world. Black people continue to trail all other races when it comes to running and operating a business. Most black people will start a company without having a clear understanding about their business, knowing their demographic of customers, or even understanding how to incorporate their company. Just because you know how to do hair, fixed a few cars, or sell knock off clothes out of your trunk, doesn't mean you know how to run a business. I remember watching television years ago and a rap artist by the name of 50 cent announced he was launching a new record label called G-UNIT Records. I said to myself, "if he could start a new record label, I could too." Even though I had no knowledge of running and operating a record label, I still insist on starting one. The record label was a total flop because I didn't have the proper education on how to run and operate it. It's even crazier how long I continued to run the label knowing I didn't have a clue what I was doing. That went on for two years.

This is not just my story, but there are many black companies running their companies without any education about their business. To prove a few facts, I had a company years ago that offered a magazine subscription service to people in the United States. Every complaint I received from my customers were about black publishers who didn't send the customers their magazines on time. Sometimes the magazines would be delayed six months later. Another fact was, I decided to support my black local record stores by purchasing CD's and DVD's. What made me just shake my head was the fact that these stores were selling bootleg CD's and DVD's. Why couldn't the owners just call the distributors and order the authentic products.

Lack of education is really hurting the black businesses and we wonder why we're losing in life. In order to stay ahead of the game, we must educate ourselves daily, personally, socially, and financially. So let's stop the "B.S.," and get with the real program. Education and understanding is the only why that you can achieve anything in this world.

My final issue concerning the lack of education is when dealing with the law. This is an issue why so many black people are locked up in prisons across the United States. What black people are not aware of is what the law states about if you don't know the law system. It states, "ignorance of the law has no merit in the courts", which means if you didn't know the crime you were convicted for only carried a 3 year max and you signed an agreement with the prosecutor for 5 years, it's not the courts fault. This is a problem that goes on every day and most black people are not even aware of it. For example, my cousin

Lamont Williams is locked up in Michigan State prison serving a life sentence for ignorance of the law. His situation was a robbery that went bad and resulted in murder. Throughout his whole trial, he was never described as the person who murdered the victim, but as the person who wouldn't cooperate with the police because he feared the murderer would come after his family. The prosecutor offered him a plea for 18 years and 2 years for someone else's gun, but he refused the offer because he didn't want to confess to a crime he didn't commit. He was later sentenced to life with no possibility of parole because he had no knowledge about the law.

Black people have this thing about, "if it don't affect me personally, then I don't want to know about it." For years I thought the same way until it happened to me. In 2002, I was accused of a crime (Criminal Sexual Conduct of the 3rd) I didn't commit. From the start I had no clue about the crime or how I was getting charged for it. The crime involved me sexually assaulting a 14 year old girl. What I did find out was ignorance of the law doesn't discriminate. So in 2003 I was convicted and sentenced to 3 to 15 years in the Michigan Department of Corrections. Although six people were in the house where the crime accured, there was no semen, and no evidence of struggle

15

or injuries to the victim. It was a total nightmare for me. What was even crazier was years later after I was convicted for the crime, I got a letter from the board of appeals stating it's a possibility that my DNA test may have been contaminated. This document came 7 years later, not to mention my judge Mary Waters was also under investigation in 2010 for allowing perjury testimony into the courts on an unrelated drug case. It was by the grace of God I was then released after fighting for my freedom for years and also after I received that document. Me going to prison was totally my fault because I didn't know how to handle that situation at the time. I had no money for an attorney or anything other than my word. I became a victim to the ignorance of the law like many others incarcerated across the United States.

For black people who want education about the law, there are many websites you can google to find free information concerning your situation. You can also consult with a reputable law firm and just ask questions for less than $100 an hour. Just don't wait until it's too late like I did and pay with your life. In my case, there was nothing my family could do for me because they didn't know where to go or who they could talk with to help my situation.

Black people let's tightin' up, and never say never, because a situation like mines could happen to you.

Reason 2

WE HAVE TOO MUCH PRIDE

Pride is a major issue when concerning my people. In fact, it's one of the main reasons why black people are losing the battle to achieve in life. I personally believe this problem with too much pride started after our ancestries were freed from slavery. Just think about it! After all those years of oppression would you want anyone to give you orders, commands, or some simple advice? Now a days the words "simple advice" is mostly confused with the words "orders or commands." Most black people I've encountered with would rather not take any advice from another black person. This is especially common in the black community because we fear each other so much.

The question I'm always shaking my head about is why would a black person receive advice from another person before his or her own race? For example, one day I called my aunt to see how she was doing, but she wasn't doing so well. She said her phone bill was too high and it may be shut off soon. The advice I gave her was to go to Best Buy and purchase a product called the Magic Jack, which is a device that allows you to connect to your internet service and attach a house phone to use the device. The fee was only for $19.99 per year with unlimited calling. She said, "are you sure, that doesn't sound right and I don't know anyone who has it." What really had me heated was I called my aunt months later and she was telling me she just seen a commercial about the Magic Jack and she was going to purchase the item. That was one of the craziest things I've ever heard. Not to mention, she never said I was right and she was wrong.

Black people we have to get over the pride issue because its' like cancer. Once it spreads it gets to our children and that can become a road block for achievements in life. I once spoke with a man by the name of Scott Mayfield who told me, "Once you got over your pride, you'll be sure to glide." That statement is so true; I can definitely witness it as a fact. My last stand with pride ended in 2003, when a singer/songwriter by the name of Patrice Williams handed me a book about "learning the music industry." My pride kicked in when the thought of a woman given me advice on how to run my business, which was a record label. I didn't say is aloud, but I didn't want her advice, not to mention one of my recording artist was over hearing everything she was trying to teach me about my label. I felt totally embarrassed about a woman having more knowledge than me about my own business. In fact, I threw the book she handed me in the back seat of my car and didn't even read it. After about a month I saw Patrice again and she was heated at me for not reading the book and demanded it back. So many years later I eventually read and learned more about the music business myself. But the taught was still in my head so I had to call Patrice and tell her how sorry I was for letting my pride get in the way of what she was trying to share with me years ago.

Don't you think all of that could have been avoided years ago if I could've just put my pride aside and receive the blessings she was trying to share with me? Yes! That's why I say too much pride can limit black people from achievements. A stubborn person with too much pride is even worst. This is the type of person that will take his or her pride all the way to the grave. Do you think President Barack Obama is stubborn or have too much pride? No, because he wouldn't be elected as the President of the United States with those issues. And how about Oprah Winfrey? Do you think she would've gotten as far as she has in her career being stubborn with too much pride? The answer is no. There's nothing wrong with having pride about yourself or your culture. The problem is having too much pride and not receiving constructive criticism. Especially for black men who stands at #1 with having too much pride. Trust me, there's absolutely nothing wrong with getting advice to help you with your personal, spiritual or business relationships. Believe it or not, it will actually help you make better decisions in life. If I would have made the decision to listen to Patrice years ago and put my pride aside, I would've had knowledge about the music industry years earlier.

I wrote this book not to put down the black race, but to up lift and highlight the things that hold us back in life. We have so many other obstacles in life; let's not add more stress to our prior situation. Having too much pride is a major concern with black people and we must change this. Once I got over this issue, I saw how my life started to change. It blew my mind because I then realized that I was holding myself back from opportunities to come. So if you know a person with these issues, don't just point your finger and laugh, sit down next to that person and explain my story to the individual. You can also give them an illustration of your past experience of having too much pride. One person at a time, this decease can be cured. Stop saying to yourself, "I don't want this person to tell everybody he or she helped me with a problem I had." I said the same statement, but deep down I knew the other person was right. I'm telling the world I made a bad judgment, so you know I'm above pride. I've even heard a black person say, "I just don't want that nigga to take credit for my success." Is that a person that's crazy or what?

Bottom line, too much pride is too much "B.S". I'm tired of my people failing because of it. If you are a black person and not an FBI agent analyzing this book trying to find out more about black people, I want you to make a commitment from this day fourth. I want you to release the plague of having too much pride and be a more open minded person. I want you to be able to receive open heartedly information, advise, or constructive criticism from any black person with no doubt. Don't think a person is always out to hurt you. If you don't receive the advice, at least do your research about the information. It also would help to contact the person that give you the advice and tell them you appreciate their input. When I called Patrice to thank her years later, she almost didn't remember the advice she gave me but she also thanked me for the thought. So let's just get this right black people and put the pride to the side. At the end of the day, you'll know that this is some real talk and something that will better your life in the future. "Kill the Pride!"

Reason 3

WE LACK OUR RESPONSIBILITIES

Having a responsibility is like a job. Once you commit yourself to this responsibility you must carry it out all the way through. It might just be me but it seems like almost every black person I've ever met either had or have a problem with their responsibilities. Either we always late with paying bills, don't have a driver's license the first but always want to drive, or just plan irresponsible. I first encountered this situation when I was a child and my father use to tell my mother he was going to pick me up on the weekends. Once many weekends went by without my father in sight, my mother just shouted in tears, "He has a responsibility to spend time with you and I'm tired of it." Unfortunately that first educational experience was very bad for me.

Through most of my life I've encountered these same situations with my family, friends, and other associates. For many reasons from supporting a child, to getting to an appointment on time has been a major lack of responsibility for black people in general. It's a shame how we could try so hard to get a job to pay our bills just to find out once we've landed the job, we never want to show up on time.

Some of us never show up at all. I remember years ago when I was a shift supervisor at KFC, and most of the black people would always show up 10 to 30 minutes late daily. I was curious to know if that was the same case with white employees, so I called a suburban KFC to ask these questions. I wasn't surprise to find out that white employees started their shifts 5 to 10 minutes earlier. I know a lot of us come to work feeling lazy, but it's a responsibility to work the time your job schedule requires.

Another responsibility issue we lack is not paying our bills on time. If our bills are due on the first of every month, why are we mailing off our bills days and sometime weeks later? What's wrong with programming ourselves to pay the bills on time? Do you even know that by paying some bills on time makes your credit score better? My mother had this problem for years. She would even sometimes take the bill money and shop or gamble it all away. The lack of responsibility even rubbed off on me from being in a household without financial guidance. For many years I had no sense of financial responsibilities until I met a beautiful lady name Tamara Hill. She worked at the bank so she taught me the principles about paying bills on time as well as managing my finances. Before I met her, my bills were never paid on time and even my child support payments were behind.

Black people we must tighten up on our responsibility. If you make a commitment, mean what you say and do what you say you're going to do. I've tighten up on my responsibilities and now I have no tolerance for anyone who's going to neglect theirs. After being so irresponsible myself for many years, I've seen how life can be much better by being a responsible person. Yes, I use to be the one who showed up at events two hours late after being paid in advance. Yes, I use to get mad at my child's mother and even quit my job just to not have the responsibility to pay child support. Any yes, as a teen I use to want to stay with my mother for as long as I could without having financial or social responsibilities. Now I have to be the person who takes the responsibilities for my actions. Just think about it! If me and you were riding in a car and I decided to rob a gas station without you knowing, wouldn't you want me to take full responsibility for the crime if we both got caught? I would take the responsibility because I didn't tell you I was going to rob the place.

Stepping up and being fully responsible for your actions are something really serious. I remember having a talk with a gentleman when I was incarcerated about selling drugs. Despite the amount of time they gave him, he didn't understand that he was being punished and held responsible for his actions. He also didn't realize he was responsible for destroying his neighborhood's financial and social economy. His whole conversation was about how some of his homies set him up. Mind you, I was in prison for a crime I never committed, but I accepted responsibility for being ignorant to the law. Look black people, it really doesn't matter whatever your situation is, just take the responsibility for your actions. Stop depending on your mother, your father, or someone else to be responsible for you all the time. Step up and be the one everybody can depend on sometimes. I know your family and friends are tired of being responsible of you, so get your shit tight. And as for responsible black women, they don't want a man that's irresponsible. The same as for responsible black men, we don't want to be bothered with an irresponsible woman. Think about it! Would you want a woman that spends all her rent money on designer shoes and handbags? Or ladies would you want a man that never spends time with his child? The answer is no. If a person settles for a person who neglects their responsibilities, it's a good chance that person is also irresponsible. For years, I hated Friend-of-the-Courts for making me pay all of that money for child support. I soon learned it was because I was neglecting my responsibilities to support my children financially. Imagine that I was so irresponsible the government had to step in and take control of the situation. The other responsibility is about raising a child, which to me by far is the most important job. Any man can father a child, but a real man raises a child.

While incarcerated I discovered there were many black men raised in a household with a single parent. 98% of the time that parent was the mother. This curse has to be put to an end. I had no male guidance other than my uncles while growing up and that's not the same as having a father in the house hold. A father under the same roof can influence a boy on how a man should be responsible and respectful. Until now, I didn't realize how important it was for me to be living under that same roof with my children. Being incarcerated really opened my eyes to a lot of things. Also while incarcerated (under the same roof with men), I discovered I had many other hidden talents about myself. Imagine that! Just think what could happen if we all just become a part of our child's household. Imagine what talent you might discover your child may have. Your child may be the next black president, the next Kobe Bryant, or even the person who discovers the cure for AIDS. I don't recommend anybody to go to prison, but I do recommend a person to be more responsible for their actions. What we as black people must strive for is the best and the best is already in us. So the next time you feel like using your bill money for other uses other than paying your bills, pay your dam bills! Or the next time you feel like going out to the club instead of spending time with your child; skip the club because it'll always be there. Being responsible is a must and we as black people must take a stand. Let's be men and women about our responsibilities and live better off.

Reason 4

WE'RE VERY MATERIALISTIC

I know there's nothing wrong with spending money but when your label as the #1 consumer of spending money on junk, that's ridiculous. Black people are spending billions of dollars a year on worthless junk. Everything from $200.00 gym shoes to $500.00 designer handbags that will be out of style the next season. We spend so much money on garbage advertisers flock to our (black people) television networks and print media to solicit their products. Come on, have you noticed the commercial ads on black network stations. How about those magazine advertisers? You would never see those same ads on another television network stations or in reputable magazines. They advertise downloadable ringtones, video games, sex enhancement products, pre-paid credit cards, and so much other garbage to get your black dollar. They won't tell you how to make money but they sure will promote their products on how to take your money.

Black people lets wake up and open our eyes. Why in the hell are we riding around the neighborhood in $5,000 cars with $20,000 worth of accessories or rockin' a $500.00 outfit without a dime in the bank. When Swizz Beatz wrote the lyrics "She Aint Got No Money in the Bank," he wasn't talking about black women. Black people just don't like having money in the bank. I really think this was programmed in our heads when we were young. You know what I mean? Who were the little girls attracted to in the hood? The little boys who had the freshest gear? Who were the little boys attracted to? The little girls who had the prettiest hairstyles. So you know just about now where all this came from, the parents! I remember picking my son up to spend the weekend with me when he was about 4 years old. I took him to Kid's Footlocker to buy him some gym shoes that he wanted. The problem was they didn't have the Spiderman shoes he wanted, so I took him to payless shoe store because they were the only store that sold Spiderman shoes. Although he got the shoes he wanted and he was happy, could you believe his mother complained when I brought him home. She asked me why I didn't buy him some Nike Air Force 1's. I told her because that's not what he wanted.

This is definitely one of the reasons why we're losing in life black people. Why are we trying to keep up with the Jones (the media) when we know we can't afford it? Why would we rather look fresh than have a roof (with running water) over our heads? My child's mother only felt that way because she may have been raised without financial education. This is also an issue my mother had. She would even spend money on things she sometimes never used. Black people, money don't grow on trees, so we must show our children how to earn it as well. And what's up with the credit issues? Why do the majority of black people have bad credit scores? We don't value money. We can work our hands to the bone for 40 hours a week, get a pay check on Friday and be broke on Saturday morning. Ask yourself? How much money do you have in your bank account or in your shoe box right now? Do you have $5.00 or $300.00? Stop playing black people; I'm going to keep it real with you. If we don't fix this soon, we're going to start to fade away just like the Indians (minus the wealth).

Even when I was incarcerated, I noticed how much family and friends would write me in within 3 months later their addresses or phone numbers would be changed. I got to a point where I stop adding their information on my list because I knew there was no stability. We're so out of control with spending money that we don't even realize it. What's really crazy is how we risk getting put in the streets oppose to paying our bills. Don't you think it will be smarter to at least profit from some of the junk we purchase? I know all the dope boys are making profits from some of their investments, but I mean "legal investments". Saving money can be as small as taking coupons to the stores, as well as investing in the money market (RIA's, saving bonds, COD's, etc.). The internet is also plentiful with websites that can offer you savings on most of the products you buy daily. Why spend $200.00 on some Jordan's at the outlet mall when you can go to the official website and save $50.00.

Black people really need to stop fronting and start saving some money for a change. And also what's up with these so called ballers? They have this reputation of spending so much money in the clubs and on material products, but are the same people with a car full of bootleg CD's and DVD's. If you are a baller like that, why couldn't you shop at the store for the authentic products? It's because you're a fake baller just frontin'. If you're a baller for real, why are you buying knockoff designer clothes? It's obvious you bought those fake products to save money, so stop frontin'. Are we forgetting we (black people) are trendsetters? The hip-hop movement showed us that. So don't let designer clothes and cars define who we are as black people. You shouldn't care what another person thinks about how you dress or how you ride. I use to care, but not anymore. If I see an outfit that I want to wear while walking in the mall, I'm buying it. I don't care if it isn't designer, I'mma make the outfit look good on me, not the other way around.

So black people if we can change the way we spend our money, it will definitely help us in the long run. Don't you know the average life span for a black person is between 70 to 80 years? Our retirement starts at age 60 so make sure you have enough funds saved up. You and I know we can't work or hustle for the rest of our lives, so let's keep it real with ourselves and start managing our money a lot better then we're doing. For example, if you just save a hundred dollars a week for ten years, you would have $52,000 in the bank. By the time you're in retirement, you would at least have $208,000 plus interest and social security (if there's any left) saved up. Some of you are already spending over a hundred dollars a week on nothing. You may not think about saving money now, but when you get older and the money runs out, you'll wish you had money saved for a rainy day. Besides, no one wants to be around an old broke person unless they have money. Do you think Anna Nicole Smith would have spent time with that old billionaire if he didn't have money? Because you have money now is why half of your so call friends are hanging around you today. Instead of treating them all out to dinner and whatever, start saving those funds and I bet you'll find out who your true friends are.

Black people we have to stop being so materialistic and learn the value of a dollar. If we don't wake up and manage our money better, someone else will. It's people lined up to take our money and use it to put their kids through college. So why you're out spending, give a big guest who you'll be working for when you turn 60. Bingo!

Reason 5

WE HAVE NO UNDERSTANDING

OF OUR HISTORY

I really felt the relevance of this issue because I believe most black people know their history, but don't understand it. I know we were taught in school or at home about our ancestors being slaves on big plantations but there's more. I know we were taught that our people had to spend many hours in the blazing hot sun, picking cotton for their slave masters but there's more. I also know we were told about how our people were wiped or killed for many other reasons but there's so much more. Those are just a few things I know we all know about our ancestors. My question to you is how did most of those things happen and why? It is kind of like, what's going on now? We were tricked (bamboozled). Our ancestors were tricked into being slaves by many countries with flashy items. Have you ever seen the movie, "Shaka Zulu?" If you haven't, rent it today. Anyway, the movie depicts how we were tricked into slavery. Once you've seen the movie you'll see how our ancestors were once a great nation. We had the most beautiful black women and the men were strong mighty warriors. The land was so rich with gold, diamonds, and materials of the earth. Once we were tricked into slavery and tricked out of our land it was over. Black people haven't been right since.

Black people, we need to understand, if we were tricked then, it's a strong possibility we are being tricked now. It's so amazing that most of the black people I've talked with feel like they'll never amount to nothing in life. I mean they just threw in the towel. It's history repeating itself over again. Black people the battle isn't over until a winner is pronounced. There shouldn't be anything in the world to stop you from being a great black achiever. Just look at history, there were many blacks defeating their oppression, later to become achievers in life. Blacks like Frederick Douglass, Harriet Tubman, George Washington Carver and Martin Luther King, Jr., these people went through tough times just like us. In fact, most of them had it much worst. So don't be trippin about how it's so hard for you, just get up off the couch and make a difference in life.

A man by the name of Martin Luther King Jr. once said, "I have a dream." The dream was about black people taking charge of their lives and overcoming the many problems he or she faces in life. That's one person that stood up for change and things really did happen. Just like that black people, you can make a decision on how to become a better person and achieve it. It's up to you if you never want to seek the education to achieve your goals. It's also up to you if you want to sit in the house, watch television and play video games until your 40 years old. Why you're wasting time on nothing, other races will be advancing to higher education, living in better communities, and inventing ways to keep you on that couch.

Malcolm X was right when he said, "We didn't land on Plymouth Rock, Plymouth Rock landed on us." Meaning, we didn't come to these places willingly we were tricked and forced into slavery. Understand your history black people. Understand that you are more precious than any jewel on this earth. Understand that you don't have to live like your living now. De-program your train of thought from impossible to possible. Stop letting people trick you into thinking you're not worth anything. I see a lot of black women falling for this all the time. I was watching an episode of the Jerry Springer show one day, and a black woman announced she was having sex with her mother's boyfriend. You mean to tell me a beautiful black woman would fall for a trick that's so obvious. The trick is to destroy your image on national television just to get a check for $50.00. Another trick is when the government set blacks up to catch felonies. This trick follows a law that states if you're a convicted felon, you can't own a gun. The plan is to disarm all black people in the United States. So when you destroy your image on shows like the Jerry Springer show, you become a person the government can now regulate. They regulate us by showing these images of us on television to prove we're dangerous people, mentally and physically.

So I can say it again black people, "We must understand our history." I never knew I could actually write a book from cover to cover until I tried. So that tells you a lot about me. You and I are the same people; we have the same dreams and desires. What we want out of life is to become an achiever and for our families to live without poverty. It's not about a bunch of jewelry, clothes and cars; it's about being stress free and not having to struggle in life. I don't know about you, but I want to grow old and watch my kids and grandchildren fulfill their dreams and goals. Black people we're not the bad images you see on television. We're great mothers and fathers, so don't let anyone tell you different.

If our ancestors are looking at us now, what do you think they're saying in heaven? I think their saying to themselves, "You mean to tell me we slaved in the hot sun, got wiped, and died for this." We owe them more than that black people. Our people took one for us and all we have to show for accomplishments is one black president. President Barack Obama played his part in stepping up, so when are we going to play ours. How long will it take for you to make your mark in history? I don't know about you, but I'm not waiting anymore. I had every excuse in the book about why I wasn't doing this and that. I soon realized it was just me stopping me. There were no walls in my way, there were only illusions. What is an illusion? It's a trick that will have you thinking something's there but it's not. Most of my life I fell for these tricks, but not anymore. Black people we're all presented with the same tricks, but if we understand our history those tricks will simply vanish.

I had to write this book because these issues were heavy on my heart. Black people you must understand where you're from to get to where you're going. There's not one thing you're going through that another black person haven't been through. We all hurt and have struggles. We all deal with the many issues of racism and segregation. We all are considered as the worst race on the earth. But if we let these things consume us, we'll never walk straight. We're a mighty nation and we have to act like it today. For my black brothers and sisters locked up, stop saying to yourselves when you get out your going to change or start your business plan. You're already in college, that's not a prison. Life is what you make it black people. When I was incarcerated I never thought of it as a prison. In fact, I wrote over 200 songs, 7 business plans, and 2 books. So don't tell me you can't accomplish anything, that's not for us black people. Understanding who you are is the key for understanding the history you're about to establish.

Reason 6

WE DON'T RESPECT SEX

For many generations black people have yet to acknowledge the growing problems in our communities concerning sex. It's like the elephant in the room because no one wants to talk about it. This is something I can't understand because among all races blacks are the #1 victims of AIDS, HIV, and STD's. I mean, if you can die from having sex wouldn't that be a real conversation you would want to talk about? For many years I had no respect for sex but now my eyes are open and I see things a lot different now. I also can see how a person can lose respect for sex. For example, when I was 14 years old I was introduced to sex by a friend of the family. She was 19 years old and also having sex with my uncle. I never approached her for sex; she approached me one night while she was sleeping over for the weekend. From up to that day I would just lie to my friends about having sex. I was so into music it never really crossed my mind to actually have sex one day. Although my mother did have conversations with me, I was never fully educated about the birds and bees. I also think I should've been taught by a man instead of a woman since I was a boy. But because of those

41

experiences, as I got older, sex wasn't something I looked at as being sacred.

Children should never be exposed to sex like I was. This is happening in the black communities all the time, generation after generation. What does this create? No respect or understanding about sex. Most young people feel it's cool for them to have sex because their parents had sex when they were young. Sorry to say it but this is the happening thing in the black communities. My grandmother had sex when she was very young. My mother also had sex when she was young. And you guessed it; I'm included in the pack. You know why? There were no foundations put in place for me to understand the consequences before I had sex. Even the schools in the black communities didn't know how to address the issues about sex. So once I got older I was like Kanye West because you couldn't tell me nothing. I can only remember one black male giving me an illustration about sex and he was a hip hop artist name Slick Rick. He released a song called "A Teenage Love," which taught me a lot more about sex awareness.

Black people, if we don't tighten up and stop the B.S., this cycle will continue to go on. All this having babies out of wedlock (without being married), orgies, and sleeping with every person in the hood have to stop. We don't even say mother or father anymore. It's "My baby daddy" or it's "My baby momma." Black people have no respect for sex. Black women in the United States are diagnosed with the most cases of HIV and AIDS (as of 2012). Out of the black men and women, the women account for 60% of all the cases in the United States. Which means, out of every 20 black women, 2 of the women may have contracted either HIV or AIDS. Personally, I think most of the women were exposed to those diseases at the hospitals and clinics while getting monthly check-ups. Although that's my personal opinion, statistics show that the women are contracting the diseases by their sexual partners. Women don't get it twisted, black men getting release from prison is not the cause of the spike in these cases. Black men with HIV or AIDS in prison only make up less than 3%. The reason why black women are contracting these diseases so fast is because they're not using protection when having sex.

Sex should be scared, it shouldn't be used for financial gain, or a sexually desire. For example, I was watching a television program one day to hear a black woman named Karrine "Super head" Steffans discuss how she was a video model and did a lot of things to get notoriety in the entertainment industry. She even wrote two books about how many men she slept with in the entertainment, sports, and music industry. This is a prime example of how our black women are settling for nothing to give away their precious jewels. Do you know when you sleep with another person your souls are bind as one flesh? If you read the bible you would understand this. Even with us black men like the basketball player Wilt Chamberlain, who claimed to have slept with over 10,000 women. You mean to tell me that these women knew of this and kept on having sex with him. I was even more surprised to hear that Ervin "Magic" Johnson contracted HIV and Wilt didn't.

Black people, just because you don't have a lot of sex partners don't mean you can't contract HIV, AIDS, or an STD. Other than a curable STD, once you have it, you have it for life. It's so crazy I witness black women purposely using sex to have babies just to collect financial assistance from the government. How about getting your x-rated ass out of the bed and get a job? Even porn stars have more common sense to get top dollar for sex. I'm not saying become a porn star; just understand that sex is not something to be toyed with. I was introduced to sex by the neighborhood whore and it totally threw my whole life off course. If I would've understood about sex then, I would've never had five children by four different women. My dream was to get married with the first women I had a child with. What happened was basically what happens in the black communities all the time, "We have sex before we even get to know a person." Once we found out who the other person actually is, we regret that we didn't get to know each other before having a baby.

We have to respect sex black people. This is something that's very serious, but we play too many games with it. If you feel like you're not going to slow down and sex is something you're going to continue to have with multiple partners, at least use protection. I know it's like smoking and it's hard to break the habit, but it's something we have to work on. We can stop the spread of these fatal diseases just by wearing protection. The cure lies in us, not scientist to find the cure for AIDS and HIV. The money is not in the cure, but in the medicine it contains. Which means you'll pay more for the medicine in the long run, verses for the cure right now. And what's up with the saying, "if a woman has multiple sex partners', she's a whore, versus a man having sex with multiple women is a hero?" If that's not the dumbest shit I ever heard. If a man has sex with a lot of women, he's a whore. I should know, because I was a whore at one point in my life.

Bottom line, we need to keep it real with each other black people. I know we have a lot of issues to confront, but sex should be at the top of the list. I want to see a lot more black people married for a change. I don't want you to tell me you're about to go over your baby momma's house to pick up your child. You know how ghetto that shit sounds? Tell me your about to take your wife out to dinner. Or how about actually going home to your wife instead of the strip club? It's a saying in the hood for non-sense and we call it nigga shit. I know the word suppose to be dead, but a lot of black people be on some real nigga shit. That's nigga shit if you have babies all over the hood. That's nigga shit if you're sleeping with multiple sex partners' without using protection. So let's keep it real with each other and respect the use of sex and all the responsibilities around the issue.

Reason 7

EVERYONE WANTS TO BE A

CELEBRITY OR BOSS

Why does it seem that every black person I've ever met wants to be a superstar or leader of something? It's cool to be a part of something but learn that shit first. This is something I just can't figure out. I've even seen some black people portray themselves as celebrities by plastering their images all over the products they were promoting. Everything from posters, to magazines, and even billboards. This is something I've even done myself. In 2002 I launched a music magazine called, "Black Life Entertainment." Although it was relevant, I was on the front cover of my own product. I even miss the opportunity to sale more magazines and ad space by putting myself on the cover instead of a well known entertainer. What mattered to me was I liked the attention I was getting from the magazine cover. I believe that's how all of us (black people) feel. We don't want anyone to forget about us.

After analyzing a lot of these issues, I now understand that everybody can't be a celebrity or a leader. Somebody has to play the role as the consumer or the student in order for life to evolve. Also, you can't just make yourself a celebrity or leader; you have to be chosen by the majority. For example, I've seen many recording artists' come in the game years ago, but now those same artists' are not as young or popular anymore. Despite the fact that their careers are over, they're still trying to appeal to the media as the young and popular artists' they once were. The only way they can get a pass by me if the artist is still selling concert tickets. Is it me or wouldn't it just be simpler to recruit some new talent and pass the torch? I mean these people have gray hairs and everything, but that still doesn't stop them. I've even seen black people rent limousines to ride around the hood just to look like a celebrity. That's called "Ghetto Fabulous."

Black people we have to dig deeper to find a better understanding about what we are trying to become. We also have to learn how to improvise. It may not be your destiny to be a superstar or a boss. Superstars and bosses are chosen by the majority. Black people we have to invest in people with these potentials instead of giving ourselves fake titles. Look at Will and Jada Smith; they're already investing in their children to become superstars. Hiring agents and managers to handle their careers at an early age, this is necessary. And it also means that it's nothing wrong with black people investing in other black people. Don't worry about your face being plastered all over your product because the credits say it all. Meaning, when people read the credit review, you're an instant celebrity. Of course most of the people will glorify the artist but the pay check will glorify you. So stop trying to be the celebrity and let your work speak for itself.

Now as for every black person trying to be a boss or a leader, cut it out! Why is it that no black person wants to follow before becoming a boss or a leader? Regardless of how much you think you know about running the job yourself, play your position. Wait until it's your time. Some black people will even force their way into the lead position without fully understand the responsibilities. For example, I overheard two artists' on my old record label (Linwood Records) years ago discuss their views about me running the label. Saying I didn't know what I was doing so they should team up and start their own record label. It was a fact I was still learning how to run a label, but it was also a fact the artists' had no clue about running a label themselves.

There are also black people who take on roles as leaders, but no one wants the responsibility. You mean to tell me you want me to follow you right into a brick wall? It's not going to happen! It's not about pride because I don't have a problem following a black person. As long as I know it's in my best interest, it's cool with me. Although, I do have a problem if you want me to sell your drugs, or if you want me to kill four people for you. That's when I'm going to look at you as an enemy, because you're trying to lead me to hell. Black people if we're going to be leaders at anything, just make sure we at least acquire the education we need about the position before giving ourselves that title.

Once you've become a boss or a leader, you would have the majority of the responsibility. That means, if you're the boss of a drug conspiracy and you get busted, you will receive the most time. And let's say you're the coach of the Detroit Pistons and you made a bad decision to take the star player out of the game, which causes the team to lose. The news headlines will read, "Bad Coaching!" So black people, sometimes it's not cool to be the leader. Also understand, I'm not trying to say, we shouldn't be leaders, I'm saying we should obtain the knowledge and skills before we decide to lead. Just because you have the knowledge and skills, don't misuse the responsibility. For example, I watched a young aspiring black man named Kwame Kilpatrick become the youngest mayor of Detroit, Michigan. He did an amazing job of bringing Detroit out of once was considered a dead city. I even thought this guy might become the next black president because he had that quality leadership that everyone wanted to follow. Although he turned the city around from destruction, his down fall came when he made a lot of bad decisions while being the leader. Those bad decisions not only destroyed his career as the mayor of Detroit, they also landed him in prison. Bad leadership took him from being mayor to becoming an inmate of the Michigan State of Corrections.

So black people believe me when I say it, being a leader takes great responsibility. This is serious because it's a lot of black people incarcerated because of the leadership role they played in a crime. We shouldn't be leading our people the wrong way. Don't you want to be the person who leads a man or woman into a position that may help you in the future? What if you need a job and the person you helped years ago is now the president of that company. Chances are you'll get hired. Now turn the tables around and guess what may happen if you cause that same person to go to jail for something you had them do for you illegally. They might call security and have you thrown out of the building

Everybody may want to lead, but the chosen ones are meant to lead. Let's stop making self-made titles and forcing ourselves into positions we didn't work for. President Barack Obama worked really hard and earned the title as "The Boss of the United States of America." So don't think being the boss is an easy task. We as black people are naturally born with leadership skills but every great leader has to follow someone. A great leader listens to his people. A great leader takes full responsibility for his actions. Also a great leader knows when to step down and let his or her student lead. Remember, I mislead a lot of people myself, so I know what I'm talking about. I'm not just saying this to hate on black people who want to become leaders or celebrities. I'm just saying don't front like you know what your doing and don't know anything. Just keep it real and say, "You're just learning how to become a leader." Trust me; life would be so much better off. I felt so much better when I told one of my artists' that I didn't know how to run a record label, but I was learning. He really respected me more when I kept it real with him.

So black people if we're going to be leaders or become celebrities, let's earn these titles. It means nothing to give yourself a title, what really matters is that someone else gave you that title. So earn your stripes and then become a boss or a celebrity.

Reason 8

WE DON'T RESPECT EACH OTHER

One saying my grandfather Oliver "OJ" James Evans use to always tell me was, "You don't have to agree with a person, but you have to respect them." That's one of the sayings that I've shared with my kids now. The problem I see in the black community is we don't have respect for each other at all. We call each other offensive bad language, and anything else to show that we don't respect one another. Most of us don't even have to know the other person personally to not have any respect for them. For example, I was watching a television program with a black man and he decided to voice his opinion about an artist (which was P. Diddy) on the television show. Out of the blue, the guy just said, "I don't like that bitch ass nigga." We weren't even having a conversation and he busted out like that. You know me; I had to ask him why. His answer was, "I heard that nigga be fucking people out of their publishing royalties."

Black people, we can't disrespect people because of something we heard about. How can you dislike or disrespect another person you don't even know. It's crazy because out of all the races I've talk with; black people are the only people who act like that. It can just be a rumor about you and that's good enough for a black person. We'll say something like, "He think he's all that because he got a new car or cause she got a new hair style." I really think the problem is that most of us have low self-esteem issues. I also really think it's because some of us lack social and creative skills, we become envious at the people who have those skills. A black man flat out told me one day he was envious of me because I could produce music better then he could. What he didn't understand was that it was only his opinion about me. Meaning, if both of us would've produced a song each, it's a chance more people would have liked the music he produced verse the music I produced.

We have to stop focusing so much on negative energy black people. We don't respect each other because we're too busy sizing each other up. I mean we'll spend hours, days, even years talking negative about another black person for nothing. Black people are the only race I know that will analyze you and find a flaw about you to talk about. This is a person that doesn't know how to socialize. These people also like to talk about negative shit (drugs, guns, hatin', etc.) because they don't know how to hold a normal conversation. So while these people are stuck in time, they feel it's their obligation to disrespect a person who has moved on. I feel that once you're an adult, it shouldn't be any reason for you to disrespect another person.

I remember when I was 15 years old; I disrespected my mother by calling her a bitch. I was out of control and I also busted out the front window on the house after she kicked my ass out of her house. Those missed-meal-cribs caught up with my ass weeks later. From that day on, I never disrespected my mother again. "Sorry momma for putting you through hell."

Also black people, just because a person doesn't have money or power, we still should respect them. Even if the person doesn't practice the same religion as you, we still must respect each other. Like my grandfather said, "We may not agree with that person, but we have to respect them." I'm from Detroit, Michigan and I love my city, but we got some of the most disrespectful black people I've ever seen. I mean it's out of control. I don't know about some cities, but "Hatin" is a word Detroiter's describe as disrespecting. If you riding a new car down the street, somebody hatin: If you just got you hair and nails done and your coming out of the salon, somebody hatin: I don't care if you're a celebrity or from another state, if Detroiter's don't like you, they hatin'. This may be because of the high poverty rate in the city. Meaning, why should we be happy about you having something we can't afford? So disrespectful!

I can relate to a lot of these issues, that's why I wanted to write about them. I had friends who had nicer shit then me but I never hated. Although those friends were fortunate to have nicer things, I didn't feel jealous or envious. For example, when I was younger I use to have some friends who lived a lot better than I did. I just said, "Since he has all the G.I Joes action figures, his crib will be our designated clubhouse." I learned at an early age that it's more convenient to have allies than to disrespect someone and create an enemy. If you know it or not, that's what you're creating when you disrespect a person. You don't know if you're going to need that person again sometime in your life. It doesn't have to be the person you've disrespected; it can be a friend of the person you disrespected that may help you.

One of the reasons why black people are losing in life is because we close the window of opportunity by disrespecting others. If you're trying to expand and explore more opportunities in life, how will you be able to by disrespecting every person you see. Stop focusing so much energy into hate and focus more on your goals. This is one of the main reasons why we can't accomplish anything. For example, one day I met a black man that said he just like to watch other blacks and analyze their behaviors. We already got the federal government doing that job, so just do you. I don't know about you but it's stressful to watch black people hurt each other all the time. Do you want to see that every day? I don't even watch television like I use to because of that. The thing is finding your nitch and building on it. It has to be something you like doing other than watching other people. You could write a book, start a business plan or just try to do something more constructive with your life.

Black people the point I'm trying to make is, we have to focus more on the goals we set to accomplish. We can't dislike or disrespect each other because we are not fortunate like others are. We have to learn to focus that negative energy and be more supportive of each other. You may not like me for some of the things I've written about in this book, but you will respect me. I respect all people. I don't have to agree on your religion, on your sexuality, or even your opinion, but I do respect you. So if we can all get on that level, we'll see how better off we could be. Like I said before, the only people holding black people down is black people. Look around you, there's no chains, no wipes, just us. We're the only people hatin' on black people. We're the only people acting like crabs in the barrel when other black people begin to elevate their lives. We're also the only races who prey on the downfall for our own people once they achieve success. So please black people, let's all be like Aretha Franklin and R.E.S.P.E.C.T. each other.

Reason 9

MOST OF US HAVE NO

SPIRITUAL CONNECTION

When I'm referring to not having a spiritual connection, I really mean not having a relationship with God. I think most black people know God, but they may only acknowledge him when times are bad. Think about it? How many times have you praised God for something he did in your life that was good? Although it's not wrong to call on God when you're in trouble, we should also give him praise when he's working good deeds in our life. I use to be a person who only called on God at bad times, but that all changed while I was incarcerated. I had no connection with God until I seen the things he wanted me to see.

This is my testimony on how I found God. When I was 17 years old, me and my cousin Lamont Williams always had dreams of becoming rich and getting our families out of the hood. I was the rapper and he was my biggest fan. The thing was, we couldn't get anyone to invest in the studio equipment we needed. Our families didn't have the resources or the money to invest in our project as well. Although we had part-time jobs on the side, we also both had babies on the way. So at this time the money we were earning wasn't enough to get the studio equipment we needed. Things were down hill until one day me, Lamont and three of my other cousins were approached by the devil about making some fast money. The devil said, "If yall help me rob this guy, I'll give everybody $1,000 each." Since robbing was so common where we stayed, we all agreed on it.

Now we all knew it was wrong, but none of us had a spiritual connection. The only thing the devil did was offer us some money and we were ready to sell our souls. The devil had everything planned out, we were like fools ready to help him. We figured that since nobody was going to get hurt, it was all good. Wrong! It's never all good when you're dealing with the devil. So that night finally came and the devil picked up everybody accept me. For some reason God didn't want me to go so he put me in a deep sleep when the devil came knocking at my door. The next day I woke up the phone was ringing off the hook. When I answered, my jaw dropped because I found out the devil had murdered the guy we had supposed to rob. What was even worst, all of my cousins including Lamont were being charged for the murder because they wouldn't cooperate with the police. My uncle Bay-Bay kept asking me did I know anything about it, I just played dumb. Sorry unk for lying!

It was just that easy, the devil gave us the bait, and we took it. This is something that happens in the hood every day, because most of our young black people have no spiritual connection, the door is right open for Satan. It was by the grace of God my three cousins were acquitted for the murder, but my other cousin Lamont didn't make it out the devil's claws. He was convicted for first degree murder and sentenced to life for a robbery. You would also think after being in a situation like that I would've found a spiritual connection with God, wrong! There was no spiritual connection or influences about God anywhere in my life. Not my mother, not my friends, there wasn't anybody. What I did find later, was where there's a God, there's a way.

I believe God has a purpose for us all on this earth. He's all around us every day. Most of the times we're so busy we don't even realize it. He wants us to get to know him but we're too busy thinking about ourselves and so many other things we don't hear him calling. Well, this is how he made me listen to what he had to say. After my cousin Lamont got locked up, the letters and money I was sending him got lighter as the years went by. Eventually, I stopped writing all together and I just gave his mother money time after time. What I didn't know was God was working through Lamont to get my attention. Since I didn't want to listen, in 2003, I was convicted for a crime I didn't even commit. I was sentenced to 3 to 15 to the Michigan Department of Corrections. Now this is when my life begins to change. Out of 50 prisons in Michigan, try to guess which prison they sent me to? Yep, the same prison in Detroit, Michigan where my cousin Lamont was housed.

Like I said before, nothing happens by accident, it's only by faith. After being in that situation and seeing my cousin for the first time in over 10 ten years, I knew God was working. I later found that my cousin Lamont was reborn and he gave his life to Jesus Christ. He was also a mime for the prison church choir for months. I was still in shock about my cousin being transformed. So after about a year I decided to come to church weekly and let God handle my situation. That ultimately was the best decision I've ever made in my life. I finally had a spiritual connection with God. Although I wasn't a bible expert, I was finally learning why God put me on this earth. Seeing my cousin Lamont was just the icing on the cake. So after five years of bounding and spending time with my born again cousin, God informed me. I had one more task. He wanted me to meet a lot of other people he transformed. So God rode me out to another correctional facility in Saginaw, Michigan so I could see some more of his many miracles.

By the time it was May of 2009 and the moment I walked into that prison I could feel the presents of God. As I walked out on the prison yard I couldn't believe my eyes. The entire yard was filled with men of God. I even recognized some of the men from the previous prison I was just at. But it was one person that stood out and I knew God wanted me to see him because he had a jacket on that read "I Love Jesus." This was one of the guys I briefly met at the other prison. He was a black man name Dana "Flex" Stevenson. It was weird because he sounded so proper when he talked. My first impression was this guy is a fake, but soon learned this guy was the real deal. God purposely sent this man my way before I was to be released from prison. So weeks later, I finally got a chance to sat down and talk with Flex. He told me his testimony and I was very shocked. The only thing I was thinking was God is the most powerful person ever. If he could change this black man and flip his life inside out, there's nothing on this earth he couldn't change.

As black people we all have to understand and build a relationship with God. There's no way your situation can be better without him. Most of my life I was taught I can make it without him, but I soon found out I couldn't. We all need God and we should all try to gain a better relationship with him. After I met Flex, he really educated me on my Savior (Jesus Christ). I mean no one ever explained it to me like he did. I also took a bible study class with New Creations Ministers in Grand Rapids, Michigan. I was amazed at how many black, white, Puerto Rican, and Hispanic men had transformed their lives through Jesus Christ. Guys like Michael L. Wilson, Reggie Johnson, Hector Santiago, Phillip Williams and many others. So after I saw the power of God in these people I knew they were transformed to testify to people like me. These guys even embraced me into the church where I was eventually chosen to play keyboard for the worship service. Although my journey with those people changed my life forever, my time was up because I was released several months later.

God has a plan for us all, but we need to open our eyes and ears. I was too busy in the streets to open my eyes and ears, so God did it for me. What I'm trying to tell you is, don't wait until you end like me to hear his voice. It's a lot of people in their graves wishing the same thing. Their saying "only if we would have just listened to his voice". A lot of things we do in life we regret, but this is mostly when we're caught. This is the time we only seem to have a spiritual connection with God. It shouldn't be like this, but most of the time it is. The question is, when are you going to change? Are you going to lose 7 years of your life like I did before a change? Are you going to get sentenced to life in prison before you change? Or are you going to get killed and go to hell before you have the opportunity to meet with God? I'll tell you like this, I would've been the one going to hell if God wasn't so merciful and graceful. He turned my life around and now I just want to be a better person. I'm not saying I'm perfect, because only Christ was perfect. I'm saying being a better father, brother, friend, and more connected in my relationship with Jesus Christ. Black people we all need this connection, so let's become better people and get God in our lives. Thank you Jesus!

Reason 10

WE DON'T CARE ABOUT OUR HEALTH

I know when you read this, your first thought is to fast forward to the next chapter, but this is a major problem and it's killing black people so I recommend you to continue reading. Of my many years on this earth, I've met a lot of black people and the majority of black people I've met seem to never be concerned about their health. We never seem to care about exercising, the foods we eat or even what our doctors recommend for us. Having a healthy lifestyle is something all black people should take seriously. If we don't take it serious, some of us might not make it to the next family reunion. One of the health issues is a "silent killer" that's on the hunt for black people called high blood pressure (HBP). This killer can harm your heart; harden your arteries and causes strokes. This killer also is stealth, so you wouldn't know it exist because it has no symptoms. This means, you could be eating chili cheese fries, and the next thing you know, your having a heart attack. HBP has been proven to also raise the risk of cognitive decline, dementia and alzheimer's disease. So as black people we need to understand that our health is really important. We should also try to lower our blood pressure to a normal 120/80 or less by adapting to a healthier lifestyle. A healthier lifestyle like exercising and eating properly may even reduce the risk of dementia. For some black people, exercising is like keeping money in the bank; we just don't like doing it. By exercising at least 30 minutes a day, including normal activities (climbing stairs, lifting, etc.), we can begin to live a healthier lifestyle.

Its crazy how this may sound simple, but statistics show black people are at the top of the charts when it comes to not living healthy. Even when we eat we tend to go crazy. We eat hog-mawls, chitlings, pig tails, pig nose and any other food that's not good for us (with a dash of hot sauce). For example, one day I was watching a gospel program on television and every choir member look like they weighed about 250 pounds or more. I know I'm not the only person watching this and thinking this, but I will address this issue. God never said in the bible we shouldn't exercise and eat healthy. In fact, God encourages us to think of our bodies as holy temples. Meaning we should not be eating ourselves to death because we know we're going to heaven.

Weighing over 250 pounds is not a requirement to become a choir member black people, so tighten up, literally. Control yourself at the dinner table and stop eating those snacks after 9:00 p.m. And for heaven sake, stop ordering all those fast foods. Stay at home and cook a healthy meal for a change. Black people I hate to give it to you like this, but this is another major concern. If you ever had a family member who was extremely ill or may have died due to unhealthy living (not eating right, not exercising, etc.), you should know better! It's like we're in denial of the possibilities that the same health concerns may affect us. I have a problem with this because we don't look at the consequences. For example, what if you have kids and you choose not to live a healthier lifestyle despite of your families' genetic history (obesity, high blood pressure, diabetes, etc.)? God forbid, but if you die as a result of not living a healthy lifestyle, what would happen to your kids?

We cannot look the other way on these issues black people. Why is it that most black women get upset when you tell them about their health? I mean I said something to a black woman about her weight and she just snapped. It went so far that she called her mother about the discussion we had. I love my black women because their all beautiful to me. The thing is, I'm concerned with some of the unhealthy behaviors we adapt ourselves to. Black women shouldn't have a problem if a person is concerned about their weight. If I was a person that didn't care what I ate and didn't exercise, it's obvious I don't care about myself, how can I care for someone else. Black women you must leave your feeling outside the door and understand someone really cares about your well being.

We must control these issues if we plan to live a natural life span. Even if this means cutting out some of the things we like. Things like eating too much salt, drinking sodas, and even those sugar treats. Basically if your stomach is bigger than your chest, that's definitely a problem. There's many ways to eat healthy and exercise and still be satisfied, but the first thing you'll need to know about yourself is your body mass index (BMI). This is determined by your height and weight, which should be 25 or less. You can calculate your BMI online by visiting www.healthmonitor.com/tools/bmi. You may also want to get your blood pressure checked to see where you're currently at. After, you can now start adapting a grocery list filled with healthy foods instead of the bad products. Foods that include: fish (which you should eat at least twice a week), whole grains (which may be wheat bread or cereals), nutrition (which may be five servings of fruits and vegetables daily), and protein (which may contain low-fat dairy products). There's also protein in vegetables, fish, poultry and meat. You can also find more about eating healthier at www.americanheart.org.

Exercising is another form of starting a healthier lifestyle and it's free so you won't need to get a membership at a health fitness club. By working out at home at least 30 minutes a day can be great for your body. There are a number of exercises you could start with. Jumping Jacks, push-ups, sit-ups, weight lifting, pull-ups, and dips are great for starting. Basketball, swimming, baseball, soccer, and other physical sports are also great for exercising. The Wii exercising video games by Nintendo may also work if you like using your whole body. Black people we must be serious about our health and take control now. We have to put down these traditional foods (Mac-n-cheese, barbeque ribs, mean greens, pork chops, etc.) and get healthy or die young. Start thinking of your body as if it was like a house with pipes. If your pipes begin to swell up and clog up inside, water won't be able to flow thru properly.

Black people I know it's hard, but it's something we all have to do. If we don't start to eat healthier and exercise regularly, we can add these issues to the list of how we are dying. Once again, we're losing the race because of us. We're losing because we feel we can do anything and nobody can tell us different. Well this is what I see different. I see us dying everyday because of ourselves. I see us blaming everybody and anything for our own mistakes because we're not willing to except the responsibilities of our own actions. When are we going to stop pointing the fingers and look in the mirror. Our time is now, so why not take advantage of it. Why should we wait until it's too late before we try to make a change?

I know we don't normally check our cholesterol, take our vitamins, even get the proper amount of sleep, but we need to start. Let's not do it for ourselves, but let's do it for our families and the entire black race. If we can make this commitment, we'll save an entire generation. So please black people, let's do this together and make a difference. This difference will not only save our lives; it will structure a foundation for our futures because we are the future. We're going to stand strong and be healthier. Now don't you feel better that you kept reading instead of skipping this chapter? I know you do!

Reason 11

WE DON'T GIVE EACH OTHER SUPPORT

This has been another issue that's causing the black race to lose in today's society. Black people don't support each other. Rather it's dealing with business or personal, we lack to lend each other a hand. Black people need to understand that if we don't support each other (in good times or bad) we can't survive. As well as supporting our black businesses, the business owners should also contribute to their surrounding neighborhoods. For example, if you're a black business owner who resides in a small neighborhood that is supported by black customers, you should also invest into that neighborhood. Whether it's buying books for school kids, purchasing real estate in the neighborhood, or donating overstock products to the Salvation Army, this is how we can support each other.

Another issue where black business owners fail is by not providing black customers with products they can afford. Meaning, if you want your business to be supported by other blacks, you must have reasonable prices as well as quality products. For example, one day I went shopping for clothes at a local black owned clothing retailer. While I was looking around I notice that their prices were higher than the stores at the mall (which were located in the suburbs). The owner couldn't explain it. Do the math black people, if you sale more products for less, you'll still come out with the same profit at the end of the day. We have to stop taking advantage of our people like that. Black business owners should know most blacks can't afford to over spend. So stop jacking up the retail prices and start remembering how things were when you stayed in that neighborhood.

Black people we have to stay real with each other. Another example is how we can say we support our black recording artists like Trey Songz, Usher, Rihanna, Lil Wayne, Dillon etc. and turn around a purchase their albums on bootleg. You know the bootleggers never pay the artist, but you still give them your hard earn money. Even with a movie producers like Tyler Perry, Will & Jada Smith, etc., you'll buy that bootleg DVD in a second. How can these artists and movie producers invest back into our black communities if you don't give them your support? The last bootleg I bought was in 2002 and it was a movie called Training Day featuring Denzel Washington. After thinking about it, I was the person who stopped my economy from growing. From that day forward I vowel to never buy illegal products again.

The backbone of black owned businesses relies on the support from me and my people. Meaning, if we don't support each other, we will not survive. Just look around your neighborhoods. Don't you notice how black own businesses just came and went. Their out of business as soon as the grand opening is over. Although some black businesses are supported by black customers, most companies close due to poor customer services. For example, I know a black owned restaurant that had a lot of loyal black customers supported it. The problems the company had was poor customer service, which eventually lead to the place closing. I mean the restaurant had no air conditioning, employees were swearing, chewing gum, the rest rooms were nasty and even the menu had misspelled words. Think about it, why would anyone want t eat at a place like that. Black people, we have to do better. If we want the support from other black people, we must be willing to meet or beat the competitor's service. We should give our black customers an incentive to come back for more business not scary them away.

As well as business, we also have to support each other as a people. For example, I was watching television and the breaking news story came on about two young music artists concerning domestic abuse. I later found out the artist names were Rihanna and Chris Brown. The story went on to allege that Chris Brown physically assaulted Rihanna. Well months later after the allegations were proven to be true, Chris Brown eventually took the responsibility for his actions and plead guilty for his assault. Now from the start I knew this was bad and I knew many blacks would be divided on this issue. First, I don't condone a man abusing a woman for any reason. This is something I've learned at the age of 18 when I found myself putting my hands on a woman. I slapped and verbally abuse my child's mother and was almost put in jail because of it. From that day, I repented and vowel to never put my hands on another woman as long as I lived. So I guess besides sharing the same b-day (May 5th) this is how my situation relates to Chris Brown. Including the fact Rihanna was assaulted, the other issue I was upset about was how black people threw Chris Brown under the bus. It was obvious there were some issues going on and he needed some help. Although there was a lot of blame, there was no talk from black people about getting Christ some mental help. Black people I know we need to be there and support the victim, but we also must help the person who committed the crime. If we don't, it may happen again to someone closer to us or even become fatal.

Supporting each other is a necessity and like I said before, through good times and bad we need to hold each other down. Even after we learn that a person has repent and is truly sorry (like Chris Brown's case), we must continue to support them both. I've seen a program on television where the victim (Rihanna) forgave Chris for abusing her. To me, that what something really big for her to do. So with that said, if she forgives him we must forgive him. Throughout the years me and my child's mother relationship has never been better, and she continues to support me all of the time.

I'm sure you're wondering why I'm telling you so much about my personal information. It's because I'm at a point in my life where if I can't relate to a problem myself, how can I be real to anyone else. How can I relate to a problem if I never experienced it? I don't want to be a person on the side analyzing an issue about something I never experienced. I want to be a person that can relate to the problem. And this particular problem is dealing with how black people don't support each other. I'm willing to step up anytime to help my people and that's something I'll take to the grave. We can move up but we must first move together. So don't just keep riding down the street if you see a black person trying to make an afford to sale his product (CDs, Bean Pies, Painting, etc.). Stop and see what he or she has to offer. You might see an opportunity to grow your business and become partners all together.

Black dreams are dying because of the lack of support we give each other. So let's change the way we give each other support. If it's business or personal, let's be there to lend our people a hand. Even if some of us make bad decisions on the way, let's correct our people and help build them back up. Think about it, if your kid makes a mistake while growing up, would you write him or her off? The answers is no black people, we would continue to support them until they grow up. So that is why we must continue to grow by supporting one another.

Supporting our friends and families are also a task we must handle. Rather it's a son needing help in school, or a daughter wanting her parents to attend her ballet recital, we have to be there. We even should be more supportive to our family and friends who may be in prison. Although their bad decisions got them locked up, we shouldn't give up hope. With your support and encouragement that person may come out to be very successful. So let's not count out our people because of their circumstances, let's count on each other for prosperity. Our journey together as black people should be proud and not to look back and say what we could have done better. Life is what we make it and if we make it together it would be so much better. Dreams are supported by people who also see the dreams. So start thinking big when your brother or sister tells you their ideas. Once we invest and give our support to those ideas, we'll unlock a whole new world.

Reason 12

WE HAVE SELFISH BEHAVIORS

We're finally at the end of the book and I couldn't finish without addressing the problems black people face about selfish behaviors. Every day we wake up and look in the mirror to see the #1 person in the world - ourselves. The day just wouldn't be right if we didn't look in the mirror a hundred times before we left the house. We love ourselves so much that we forget that there are other people on the planet. Everything has to be centered around us, day and night. This is nothing but a selfish behavior. I've met so many selfish black people its ridiculous. They don't care about other people because it's all about satisfying them. I don't know how most of us got like that but this clearly is a problem we need to work on.

The first issue I want to discuss about selfish behaviors is how most black people don't give back to those in need. The bible says that we should always give to the poor and the ones in need. Meaning, if you're fortunate to have a little extra money sometimes to go to the mall, why not donate some money to a charity. I've even seen black celebrities spend millions of dollars on jewelry and cars. Do you know how many kids you can feed or educated with a million dollars? Or do you know how many homes can be rebuilt in the poverty struck neighborhoods we came from? This also applies to the middle class black people in the hood. If you can afford to put thousands of dollars into a car or truck, you can afford to donate $500 to charity. It shouldn't always have to be about what we want. For example, when I was incarcerated I was walking the track and I overheard a white man talking about how he needed to work some extra hours to send his daughter some money for a computer. Although it would take him two months of work at the prison unicorn factory to earn that money, he was thinking about the needs of his daughters. That's crazy because the whole time I was incarcerated, I never heard black men discuss the same gratitude. It was more about trying to get money from their family and friends at home.

This is why we have to change our selfish behaviors. Life is not all about receiving, it's also about giving. Receiving and giving can also be as much as some advice or information about how to start a business. For example, I had a discussion with a black man one day about starting a tax preparation company. Since this person had prior experience with his own tax preparation company, I felt that he could give me some helpful advice. Thinking this guy would only give me the basic steps because of the competition, we talked for hours and he told me everything about starting a tax preparation company. This person was clearly not a selfish person. He didn't have to give me any information about starting a business, but he did. This is definitely an example of how black people suppose to network. We should be humble and willing to help each other succeed in life. That brother had no problem helping me and I know God will bless him in the future. We all can get blessed just as well as if we stop thinking of ourselves all the time and start thinking about others.

Another issue about selfish behaviors we need to deal with is contributing to our child's education for the future. I know a lot of black people were misfortunate about having proper education, but we don't have to extend this problem to the next generation. So instead of collecting extra bills (cable TV, cell phones, credit cards, etc.) we don't need, we can open up a trust fund and contribute to our child's future education. You don't have to be rich to start a trust fund for your child, you just have to sacrifice. You can contribute as much as $20 a week, which will comes out to $1,040 a year. By the time your child starts college (starting from grade school and completing high school) they'll have $12,480 in the trust fund. Some black people spend that amount on clothes per year. Black people we have to expand our minds a little bit more. Just think about it, if we invest in our child's education, maybe they want have to struggle as hard as we did. They may even land a job that will bring in so much money that they can afford to help you out in your current situation. Thinking about ourselves all the time is something that can create a problem for our future generation. So we need to do better black people.

I was once told by my grandfather Oliver "OJ" James Evans when I was young that if I had all the toys, I would be the only person having fun. He went on to say that the other kids also wouldn't like me because I was selfish. So after that speech I gave some of the toys to other kids and we all had a great time. It was just that simple, I wasn't just thinking about myself for a change and my relationships with others begin to change. The lesson to be learned about this story is how to think about the needs of others. I could've kept all of the toys, but I also could've lost a lot of friends. When we were kids those morals should have been taught to all of us. If my grandfather didn't teach me those morals I might have turned out to be a selfish person today. So we need to educate our children early in life about selfish behaviors.

The final issue I want to address about selfish behaviors is about leaving something behind when you're gone. I don't think this is an issue black people like to talk about, but I'm referring to when were died. Meaning, when we die, what will we pass down to others? There's one thing I've noticed about black people is we don't think about what if we die tomorrow. If you die tomorrow will your family have to pay for your funeral or did you get life insurance? The reason I ask that question because this happens all the time. A person dies without leaving his family any funds for the funeral expenses. To me that's a person that is selfish all the way to the death. Having life insurance should be a payment you make before a cable bill. Meaning, if you can afford to pay $39.99 a month on cable, you can afford to pay $10.00 a month for life insurance. The money from your life insurance policy should not only be enough to pay for your funeral, but also any debts you may owe. I already know what you're thinking black people, since he or she is dead why should we pay off their debts? Because some debts may carry over to the next to kin. For example, when Michael Jackson died his family inherited his estate. Although his estate had value, the family also inherited his debt, which was valued more than his estate at that time. So bottom line black people, we have to think about others in life and in death. You know you can't take them alligator shoes with you when you go, so cash them in and get some life insurance.

For so long many of us know the reasons way were so selfish, but we just don't talk about it. I was one of those people who stood on the side and didn't say anything. One day I got so tired of watching all these things happen to my people and I said, "Enough is enough." Enough with having our children fall behind in school, enough with us having too much pride that it's hurting us, enough with us lacking our responsibilities, enough with us being so materialistic, enough with us not understanding about our history, enough with us not respecting sex, enough with us trying to be so controlling, enough with us not respecting one another, enough with us not having God in our lives, enough with us not being healthy, enough with us not giving each other support, and finally, enough with the selfishness. I'm fed up just like other black people but the only way to change is if we all take the steps to change. One person can't do it alone, so let's stop the bullshit and get down to reality.

A man by the name of Ernest C. Davis told me one day that if we can get pass the word P.O.V.E.R.T.Y (People On Vicious Economical Regression Throughout Years) we can all make a difference. Black people let's stop the selfishness and let's make a difference.

Casino Da Producer

I been through so much

in my lifetime.

The Struggle...

The Slain...

The Love…

The Pain.

I will keep fighting...

for a Brighter Day ahead.

Thank you Jesus for all the

Blessings you give me.

MOCY PUBLISHING, LLC

MOCY PUBLISHING, LLC
BOOKS, EBOOKS, MUSIC & MORE!

TWELVE REASONS WHY BLACK PEOPLE ARE LOSING IN LIFE
By
Donele "Casino" Bailey

NEW

This is a powerful book filled with information that describes how black people are failing to achieve their goals in life, personally, socially, spiritually, and financially. As well as highlighting the problems why black people are failing in life, this book will also describe the steps on how to correct the problems. If you would like to become a better achiever in life, read and understand the TWELVE REASONS WHY BLACK PEOPLE ARE LOSING IN LIFE.

Life is about change and knowledge is the key. So stop playing games with your life and receive the blessings God have in store for you. Tomorrow is a new day and by reading this book you'll find a new purpose for living.
By Donele "Casino" Bailey

Price: $14.99 (Paperback)
Available: September 11, 2012
ISBN: 978-0-9834700-0-7
Item #: MPB7165

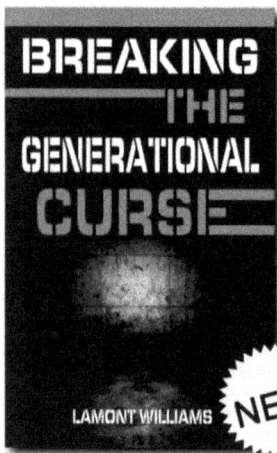

BREAKING THE GENERATIONAL CURSE
LAMONT WILLIAMS

NEW

Do you feel like you've been chained down all your life and something has been holding you back from your success in pursuing your dreams? Have you been affected by what someone have said or done to you, to the point of where you're unable to move forward with your life? Are you feeling held back in this world and no matter how much you try to move forward you end up back where you started?

BREAKING THE GENERATIONAL CURSE will show you how to break free from any curse in your life. This book will give you insight on how to overcome the past things that held you back in your life. This book will also allow you to overcome those struggles that we face in our everyday lives. You can take your life back and you don't have to be chained down anymore. Your change can start today! *By Lamont "Willy" Williams*

Price: $14.99 (Paperback)
Available: September 25, 2012
ISBN: 978-0-9834700-4-5
Item #: MPB7166

Order Your Copy Now at
www.mocypublishing.com
or Mail a Check or Money Order with order form below:

QTY	ITEM #	DESCRIPTION	EACH	PRICE
	MPB7165	12 Reasons Why Black People are Losing in Life	$14.99	
	MPB7166	Breaking The Generational Curse	$14.99	
	Make Payable to: Mocy Publishing, LLC 220 Bagley St. (Suite 1018) Detroit, MI 48226-1400		Shipping	$4.00
			Total	

www.ingramcontent.com/pod-product-compliance
Lightning Source LLC
Chambersburg PA
CBHW071138280326
41935CB00010B/1282